La

[A Maths]
JOURNEY
$<=\sim\pm\div$ ⟩around a⟨
Deep Sea
Adventure

CONTENTS

go figure

Stand by to plunge beneath the waves as you use your mathematical skills to study and explore the ocean depths.

LEARN ABOUT IT **NEGATIVE NUMBERS**

This section will take you through the mathematical ideas you'll need to complete each mission.

The practical examples in this section will test your knowledge of the ideas you've just learnt.

⟩GO FIGURE!

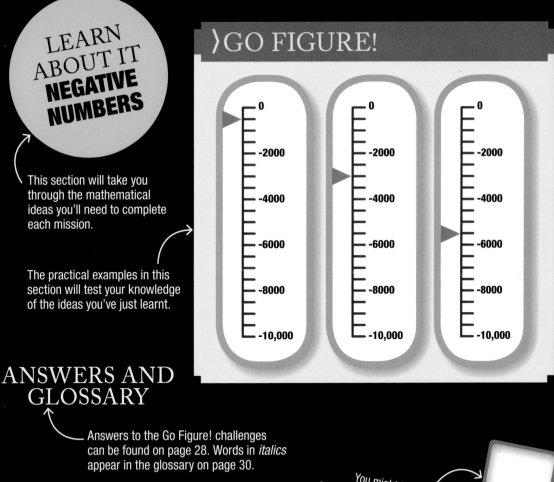

ANSWERS AND GLOSSARY

Answers to the Go Figure! challenges can be found on page 28. Words in *italics* appear in the glossary on page 30.

You might find some of the questions in this book are too hard to do without the help of a calculator. Ask your teacher about when and how to use a calculator.

WHAT EQUIPMENT DO YOU NEED?

Pen or pencil   Notepad

LEARNING TO DIVE

Your first mission is to make sure you are ready to dive, so you can explore the underwater worlds safely.

LEARN ABOUT IT
NEGATIVE NUMBERS

Negative numbers are numbers that are less than zero. *Positive numbers* are numbers that are greater than zero.

If sea level is at zero then each metre below sea level can be described as a negative number. One metre below sea level is -1, two metres below is -2, and so on.

04

Watch out! For positive numbers, 20 is lower than 30, but for negative numbers -20 is higher than -30. Find the numbers on the number line to check.

When diving or rising from an underwater position, count up or down the number line. For example, if you are at -20 m and dive five metres lower, count down from -20 to -25.

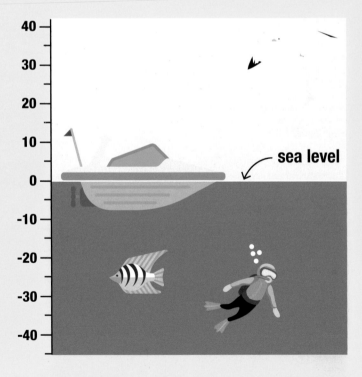

sea level

When finding the difference between two negative numbers, the answer will be the same as if they were both positive. For example, the difference between -30 and -5 is the same as the difference between 30 and 5, which is 25.

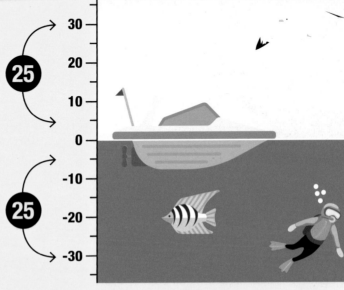

〉GO FIGURE!

It's important to know how far below the surface you are when diving, so check out these dives and answer the questions.

1 Here are some depths below sea level: -6 m, -32 m, -18 m, -40 m, -25 m a) Which of these is the deepest? b) Put them in order, from highest to deepest.

2 **You dive down to a depth of -35 (35 metres below sea level). a) If you rise 10 metres, where are you? b) From your new position, you dive a further 17 metres. Where are you now?**

3 You are at -28. If you want to get to -7, by how many metres must you rise?

4 **An octopus is at -31. How many metres is the octopus below you if you are at: a) -3? b) -16 c) 2 metres above sea level on the boat?**

CORAL REEFS

Your first dive takes you to coral reefs, endangered places teeming with life. Measure the reefs, and note any changes that have occurred.

LEARN ABOUT IT

PERCENTAGES AND PERCENTAGE CHANGE

Percentages **(%) are fractions with the *denominator* 100, so 75% =** $\frac{75}{100}$

We can use percentages to describe fractions in a way that makes them easier to compare.

To compare the fractions $\quad \frac{3}{4} \quad \frac{160}{250} \quad \frac{63}{90}$

change them all to percentages by dividing the *numerator* (the top number) by the denominator (the bottom number) and then multiplying by 100. So…

$\frac{3}{4}$ **as a percentage is 3 ÷ 4 x 100 = 75%**

$\frac{160}{250}$ **is 160 ÷ 250 x 100 = 64%**

$\frac{63}{90}$ **is 63 ÷ 90 x 100 = 70%**

We can easily see that 75% is greater than 70% and 64%, so ¾ is the largest fraction of the three.

To compare how much things have changed, find the percentage increase or decrease for each situation, like this:

$$\frac{\text{(Difference between the original amount and the new amount)}}{\text{Original amount}} \times 100$$

So, if a piece of coral 10 cm in length grew to 12 cm, the percentage increase is:

$$\frac{12-10}{10} \times 100 = 2 \div 10 \times 100 = 20\% \text{ increase}$$

⟩GO FIGURE!

You must collect data in order to compare *areas* of coral reef now with those in the past, giving the figures as percentage increases or decreases. You are visiting three different reefs, making a note of the data from 1999 and measuring the area of each reef today.

REEF A

1999	Today
250 km^2	200 km^2

REEF B

1999	Today
320 km^2	224 km^2

REEF C

1999	Today
900 km^2	495 km^2

1. Have the reefs increased or decreased in size between 1999 and the present day?

2. **What is the difference in area, in km^2, between 1999 and the present day for: a) Reef A b) Reef B c) Reef C?**

3. Find the percentage decrease for each reef, using the formula:

$$\frac{\text{(Difference between the 1999 and the present day areas)}}{\text{The 1999 area}} \times 100 =$$

4. **Which reef's area has had the greatest percentage change?**

5. There used to be around 400,000 km^2 of coral reef on Earth but there is now only about 280,000 km^2. By what percentage has the total amount of coral reef decreased?

SHIPWRECK

For your next adventure, dive down to the seafloor to explore a shipwreck and search for lost treasure. Learn how to chart the items using coordinates.

LEARN ABOUT IT
FOUR-QUADRANT COORDINATES

A coordinate grid can be divided into four areas called *quadrants*. The centre of the grid, where the x and y axes cross, is known as the origin.

You can refer to any point by giving its *coordinates*. All coordinates are measured from the origin.

Coordinates are two numbers in brackets. The first shows the distance you have to go across on the x-axis. The second shows the distance you have to go up or down on the y-axis.

The point (x, y) on the grid here is at (3, 4) because, from the origin, you go 3 squares to the right and 4 squares up to reach the point.

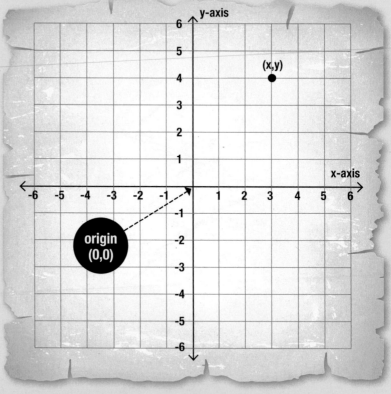

All points on the right of the y-axis have positive x values. All points on the left of the y-axis have negative x values. All points above the x-axis have positive y values. All points below the x-axis have negative y values. So (5, -3) is to the right of the y-axis and below the x-axis.

Can you locate items around the shipwreck and collect *data* about their positions?

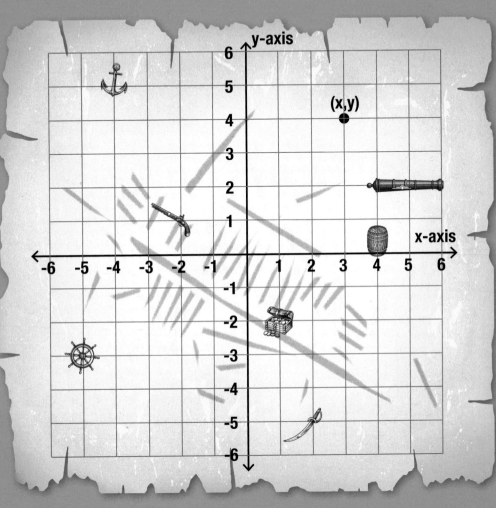

1. You must chart the items that you find at each location by writing their coordinates. Write the coordinates of:
   a) The anchor b) The ship's wheel
   c) The cutlass (sword) d) The barrel.

2. **Write what is at:**
   a) (1, -2) b) (-2, 1).

3. The cannon lies across three points on the coordinate grid. Write all three points.

4. **On your dive you have reached the point marked (x, y). How many squares left and how many squares down must you move to reach the ship's wheel?**

5. From (x, y) describe what you reach if you move:
   a) Left 2 squares and down 6 squares.
   b) Right 1 square and down 2 squares.

OCEAN BED

Still down at the bottom of the sea, you must now use sonar equipment to measure the different depths of the ocean floor. Sonar sends out pulses of sound and records when the echo returns.

LEARN ABOUT IT
GRAPHS AND AVERAGES

When reading information from bar-line graphs, make sure you know what each interval in the scale is worth.

For example, on the opposite graph, each small interval on the vertical axis can be found by dividing 1000 by 5, so each is worth 200. To find the depth of a sonar reading, look across from the end of the bar to the left-hand axis and work out what value it is level with.

The *mean average* gives us a number to summarise a set of numbers. To calculate the mean average of a set of numbers, add them all together and then divide by how many numbers there are.

For example, the mean average of the numbers 4, 7, 2, 9 and 8 is found by adding them all together:

$$4 + 7 + 2 + 9 + 8 = 30$$

and then dividing by how many numbers there are, which is 5:

$$30 \div 5 = 6$$

The mean of the numbers is 6.

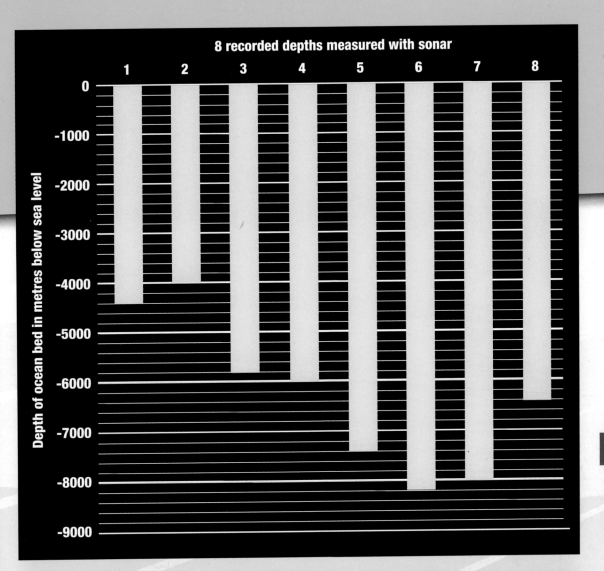

8 recorded depths measured with sonar

Depth of ocean bed in metres below sea level

〉GO FIGURE!

You have taken sonar readings at eight different points, each 1 km apart. Your readings of the depth of the ocean bed are shown on the bar-line graph above.

1. Make a list of the depth of the ocean for each of the eight sonar readings.

2. How much deeper is the ocean at:
   a) Point 6 than point 2?
   b) Point 7 than point 4?

3. Find the mean average for the eight readings.

4. Which sonar reading is closest to this mean average and therefore the most representative?

SUBMARINE

For the deepest part of the sea, you really need a submarine or a diving pod to get down to the depths. You must learn to read the dials on the control panel and how to work out your underwater speeds.

LEARN ABOUT IT
READING DIALS, CALCULATING SPEED

When reading dials and scales, count the number of intervals between each of the numbers marked on the scale. Divide the number of intervals by the difference between adjacent numbers.

12

Knots

20

B

A

0

On the dial to the left, there are 10 intervals between the numbered marks 0 and 20.

The difference is 20 − 0 = 20 so we divide 20 by 10 to give 2. Each interval is worth 2 *knots*, so A is the speed of 4 knots and B is the speed of 16 knots.

A knot is the unit of speed commonly used in maritime navigation. It is a speed of one nautical mile per hour. We can calculate average speed by dividing the distance travelled by the time taken to travel that distance.

So if we go 45 nautical miles in 3 hours, the average speed is

45 ÷ 3 = 15 knots

Speeds can also be given in other units, such as miles per hour or kilometres per hour, depending on what unit the distance is given in:

If we travel 136 kilometres in 8 hours, the average speed is

$$136 \div 8 = 17 \text{ kilometres per hour (17 kph)}.$$

⟩GO FIGURE!

As the submarine pilot, you must take readings from the dials on the submarine bridge.

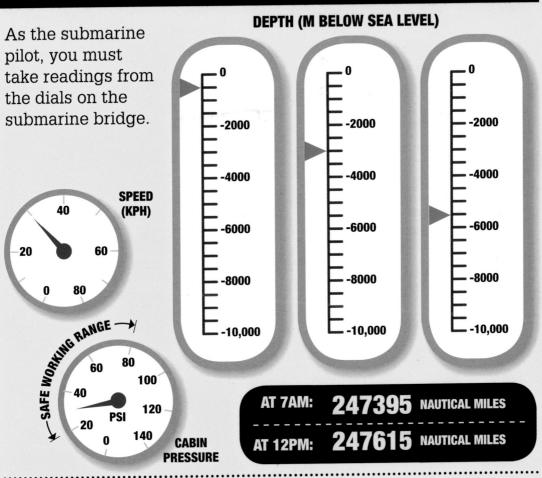

DEPTH (M BELOW SEA LEVEL)

SPEED (KPH)

SAFE WORKING RANGE

PSI

CABIN PRESSURE

AT 7AM: **247395** NAUTICAL MILES

AT 12PM: **247615** NAUTICAL MILES

1 Find the *value* of: a) The red arrow on the speedometer b) The three depths, shown on the depth gauges.

3 How many nautical miles has the submarine travelled between 7am and 12pm?

2 a) What is the upper limit of the safe working range shown on the pressure gauge? b) What is the pressure shown by the arrow?

4 Use your answer to question 3 and the length of time between the two readings to calculate the average speed in knots.

WATCH OUT!

In the underwater world, you must avoid hazards, such as other submarines. Learn how to plot a route that avoids potential dangers.

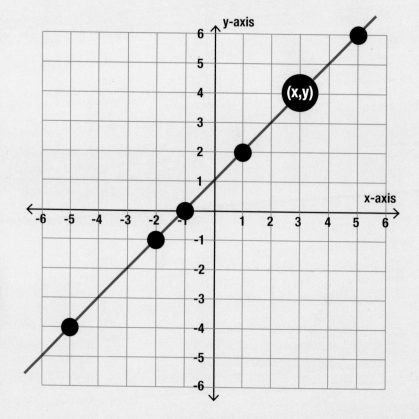

LEARN ABOUT IT
LINEAR GRAPHS

Linear graphs are straight lines shown on a coordinate grid. The coordinates of each point along the straight line share something in common.

14

Look at this line. Here are some coordinates of points along it: (-5, -4) (-2, -1) (-1, 0) (1, 2) (3, 4) (5, 6)

Can you see a pattern? The y-coordinate is always 1 more than the x-coordinate.

We can describe this line using the *equation*

y = x + 1

as every point along its length follows this rule.

We can also predict whether other coordinates are along this line or not. For example, (6, 3) is not on this line as the y-coordinate is not one more than the x-coordinate.

⟩GO FIGURE!

There is another submarine heading your way. Will your submarine lie in its path? Can you plan a submarine route that avoids a collision?

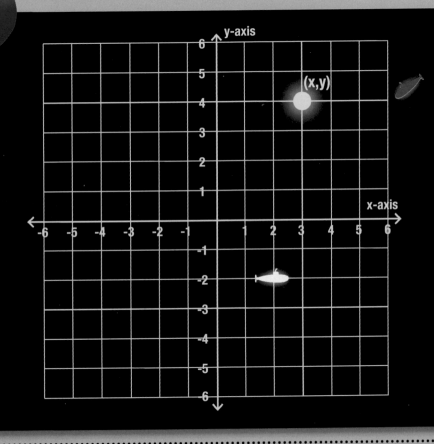

1 Another submarine is following a path using the equation $y = x - 2$. Complete these pairs of coordinates so that each shows a point along the submarine's path: a) (5, _) b) (3, _) c) (-2, _) d) (-4, _)

2 **If your submarine is at (2, -2) will it collide with the other submarine or not?**

3 Which of these submarine path equations would hit the submarine at (2, -2)? $y = x - 3$, $y = x + 4$, $y = x - 4$, $y = x$

4 **A submarine is following a path using equation $y = 2x$. Which of these points would the submarine pass through? (4, 8) (2, 0) (1, 2) (0, 0) (6, 3) (-1, -2)**

SHOALS AND SHARKS

In the deep sea, sharks hunt large numbers of fish. For this mission, find out what proportion of each shoal is eaten by each shark.

LEARN ABOUT IT
PROPORTIONS AS FRACTIONS AND DECIMALS

A proportion compares part of something with its whole. For example, in a test someone might score 7 (part) out of 10 (whole).

We can write this proportion as a fraction, $\frac{7}{10}$, or as a decimal, **0.7**. Similarly, scoring 19 out of 100 is the fraction $\frac{19}{100}$ and the decimal **0.19.**

units	tenths	hundredths
0 .	7	

units	tenths	hundredths
0 .	1	9

Sometimes we can *simplify* a fraction. For example, the numerator and denominator of the fraction $\frac{14}{20}$ can both be divided by 2, giving the simplified fraction $\frac{7}{10}$.

There are two ways of changing a fraction to a decimal. One is to divide the numerator by the denominator. For example,

$$\frac{3}{8} = 3 \div 8 = 0.375$$

The second way is to change the fraction to an equivalent one with the denominator as 10, 100 or 1000. For $\frac{3}{20}$, multiply both 3 and 20 by 5 to get the equivalent fraction $\frac{15}{100}$, which is the decimal **0.15**

⟩GO FIGURE!

Use the figures below to find out what proportion of each shoal the sharks eat.

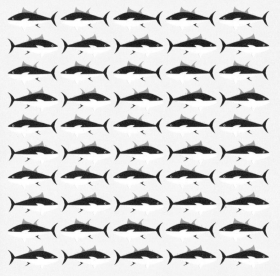

This shoal has 50 tuna.

This shoal has 100 anchovies.

This shoal has 144 herring.

1. A great white shark eats 15 tuna from the shoal. a) What fraction of the shoal of tuna is this? Simplify your answer, if you can. b) What is this proportion as a decimal?

2. **A black-tipped shark eats 90 anchovies from the shoal. a) What fraction of the shoal of** anchovies **is this? Simplify your answer, if you can. b) What is this proportion as a decimal?**

3. A silvertip reef shark eats 36 herring from the shoal. a) What fraction of the shoal of herring is this? Simplify your answer, if you can. b) What is this proportion as a decimal?

SUNKEN CITY

You've been told that the remains of a submerged ancient city are located deep beneath the sea's surface. Your mission is to chart the area and calculate the dimensions of this underwater ruin.

LEARN ABOUT IT
AREA AND PERIMETER

The *perimeter* of a shape is the distance all the way around its edge. The perimeter of a *rectangle* is found by adding the length to the width and doubling it.

The perimeter of the yellow rectangle below is:

(2 cm + 6 cm) x 2 = 16 cm

The area of a shape is the amount of surface inside it. The area of a rectangle is found by multiplying its length by its width. For the yellow rectangle, its area is:

2 x 6 = 12 cm²

If finding the area and perimeter of a shape made from rectangles, we sometimes need to find missing lengths, such as the unmarked blue and red sides here.

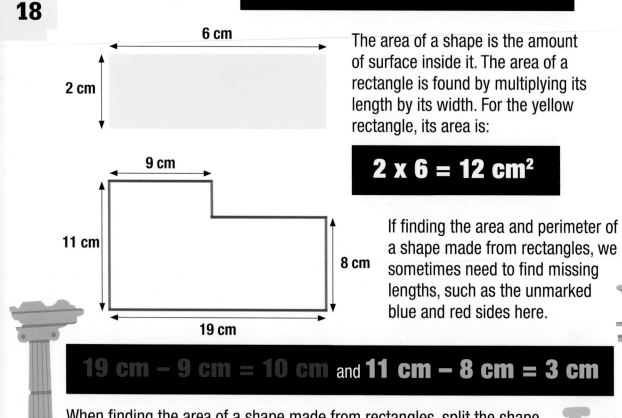

19 cm – 9 cm = 10 cm and **11 cm – 8 cm = 3 cm**

When finding the area of a shape made from rectangles, split the shape up into rectangles and then find the area of each part separately.

18

⟩GO FIGURE!

You have used underwater equipment to measure the sizes of the city's ruined buildings and have sketched some of them on this chart. Use your knowledge of area and perimeter to gather more information on the sizes of the remains.

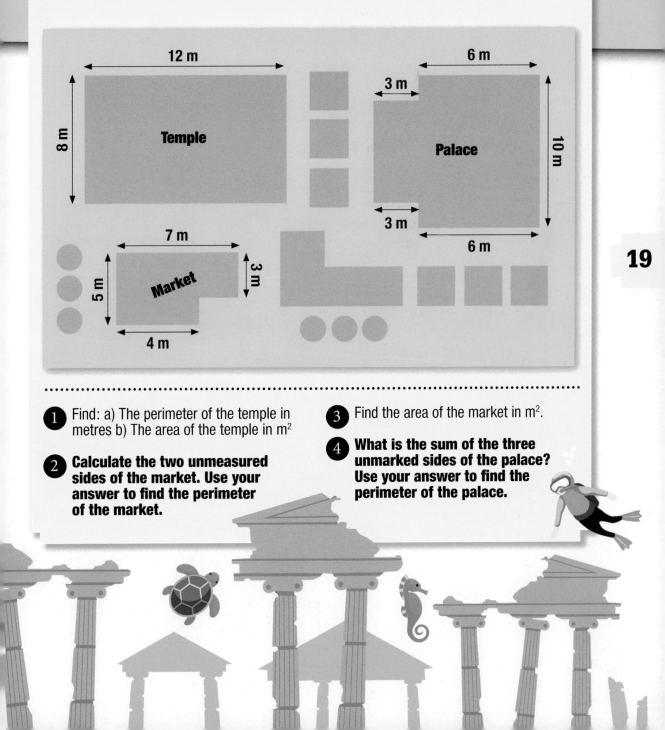

1. Find: a) The perimeter of the temple in metres b) The area of the temple in m²

2. Calculate the two unmeasured sides of the market. Use your answer to find the perimeter of the market.

3. Find the area of the market in m².

4. What is the sum of the three unmarked sides of the palace? Use your answer to find the perimeter of the palace.

WONDERFUL WHALES

Next up, you'll have a close encounter with a huge whale. It is migrating on an epic journey from the North Pole to the Equator where it will give birth.

SURFACE AREA TO VOLUME RATIO

The *surface area* of an object is the amount of surface it has. The volume is the amount of space the object takes up.

For cube A, where each of its 6 faces is 1 square centimetre, or 1cm^2, its surface area is 6 cm^2.

The *volume* of a cube is found by multiplying the length by the breadth by the height.

$$V = lbh$$

20

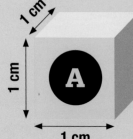

1 cm
1 cm
1 cm
A
1 cm

The volume of cube A is
1 x 1 x 1 = 1 cm^3
Notice that the surface area to volume for this cube is in the *ratio* 6:1.

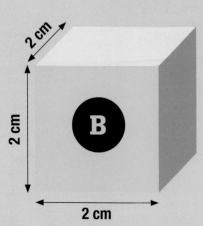

2 cm
2 cm
2 cm
B
2 cm

For cube B, where each of its 6 faces is 4cm^2, its surface area is 24 cm^2. Its volume is 2 x 2 x 2 = 8 cm^3, so the surface area to volume is in the ratio 24:8.

Like fractions, we can simplify ratios by dividing both numbers by the same number, here by 8, so 24:8 is the ratio 3:1.

⟩GO FIGURE!

C — 3 cm × 3 cm × 3 cm

Large adult whales can survive in cold waters for a long time but smaller baby whales cannot, so whales migrate to warmer waters in order to give birth. Find out why smaller whales cannot survive in cold waters by exploring the surface area to volume ratio for smaller and larger objects.

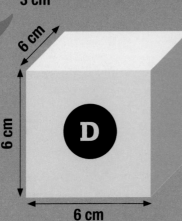

D — 6 cm × 6 cm × 6 cm

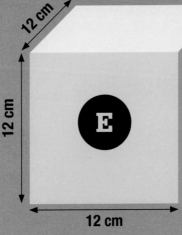

E — 12 cm × 12 cm × 12 cm

1. For each of the cubes C, D and E, find the surface area to volume ratio, simplifying them to the form _ : 1.

2. Which of the five cubes (A to E) on these pages has: a) The ratio of 1:1? b) The largest surface area to volume ratio? c) A ratio where the surface area to volume ratio is 1:2?

3. Is it true to say that the smaller the cube, the larger the surface area to volume ratio?

4. Given what you have discovered, why do you think baby whales get colder quicker while larger adults hold on to their inner heat more easily?

BILLIONS OF KRILL

Now head into a massive swarm of krill – small, shrimp-like creatures that occur in their *billions* in the ocean. Use you knowledge of large numbers to help you count them.

LEARN ABOUT IT
LARGE NUMBERS

When describing large numbers we group the digits in threes, which we often mark using a comma or a space e.g. 51 000 000 or 51,000,000.

Billions			Millions			Thousands			Ones		
HB	TB	B	HM	TM	M	HTh	TTh	Th	H	T	U
				5	1	0	0	0	0	0	0
		2	3	0	0	0	0	0	0	0	0

fifty-one million

two billion, three hundred million

When numbers have lots of zeros we can use something called *standard form*, which is based on powers of 10. When 10 is multiplied together many times we can write them using a power, like this:

$$10,000 = 10 \times 10 \times 10 \times 10 = 10^4$$

$$1,000,000 = 10 \times 10 \times 10 \times 10 \times 10 \times 10 = 10^6$$

Notice how we have written the column headings below:

Billions			Millions			Thousands			Ones		
10^{11}	10^{10}	10^{9}	10^{8}	10^{7}	10^{6}	10^{5}	10^{4}	10^{3}	10^{2}	10	1
				5	1	0	0	0	0	0	0
		2	3	0	0	0	0	0	0	0	0

This can be written as 5.1×10^{7}

This can be written as 2.3×10^{9}

⟩GO FIGURE!

As you discover the huge number of krill in the ocean, you'll need to know how to write very large numbers without using lots of digits. Krill are just 5 cm in length, but there are so many of them in our oceans that they form a huge part of the global food chain.

Recent estimates:

Number of people on the planet:	7,000,000,000
Mass (in kg) of all the Atlantic krill around Antarctica:	900,000,000,000
Mass (in kg) of krill born each year:	490,000,000,000
Total number of individual krill in the world:	800,000,000,000,000
Area (in km²) where krill are found in the summer:	19,000,000

1 Write in digits which of the numbers above is:
a) nineteen million
b) nine hundred billion
c) eight hundred *trillion*

2 How many billions of kilograms of krill are born each year?

3 Write the estimated area (in km²) where krill are found in the summer in standard form.

4 Write the estimated number of people on the planet:
a) in words
b) in standard form.

5 What is the total number of krill in the world, when written in standard form?

23

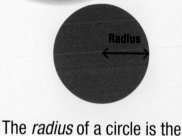

UNDERWATER VOLCANO

Your next mission, to measure the size of an underwater volcano, is your most dangerous yet. Molten lava is erupting all the time and super-heating the water around it.

LEARN ABOUT IT
CIRCLES AND CONES

First you need to learn about a special number, called pi, which we use to work out the *circumference*, *diameter*, area and volume of circles and cones.

24

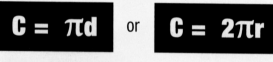

Radius

Diameter

Circumference

The *radius* of a circle is the distance from the edge to the centre of the circle.

The diameter is the widest distance across the circle, through the centre.

The circumference is another word for the perimeter of the circle.

There is a special relationship between the diameter of a circle and its circumference. For every circle the circumference will always be 3.1412… times the length of the diameter. We call this number 3.1412… *pi* and write it like this: π.

Here are some formulae:

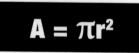

C = πd or **C = 2πr** which can be used to find the circumference C, using the diameter, d, or the radius, r.

A = πr² gives the area, A, of a circle using the radius, r.

$$V = \tfrac{1}{3}\pi r^2 h$$

is the volume, V, of a *cone* using the radius, r, and the height, h.

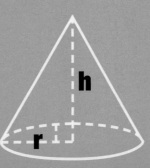

⟩GO FIGURE!

You travel around the edge of the cone-shaped volcano and estimate that its diameter at the base is approximately 6 km. You estimate that its height is about 700 m.

700 m

6 km

25

1. What is the approximate radius of the volcano?

2. **Taking π to be 3.14, find the approximate circumference of the volcano, to the nearest km.**

3. Using your answer to question 1 and taking π to be 3.14, find the approximate area of the base of the volcano.

4. **What is the height of the volcano in km?**

5. Calculate the approximate volume of the volcano, given all the other information.

6. **One of the largest volcanoes in the world is Piton de la Fournaise on Réunion Island. The diameter at its base is 220 km and it is about 6 km tall. What is its approximate volume?**

DON'T GET THE BENDS

Your final mission is to return to sea level safely! The changes in pressure that take place when you rise to the surface can be very dangerous if you go too quickly. Divers always ascend slowly so they don't get a sickness called the bends.

LEARN ABOUT IT
FORMULAE AND SUBSTITUTION

An algebraic formula is a short way of showing relationships between two or more things. Formulae usually use letters to stand for the different things.

There's a formula that will help you calculate the time you must take to ascend to the surface of the ocean safely without getting the bends.

26

$N = 6D$ shows the relationship between the number of seconds, N, you must take to rise through a given depth, D, in metres. 6D means 6 x D. We can substitute a number into the formula to find the other value.

So, to rise from a depth of 110 m below sea level you must take 660 seconds:

$$N = 6 \times 110 = 660 \text{ seconds}$$

This time can then be converted into minutes and seconds.

$$660 \text{ seconds} = 11 \text{ minutes}$$

Remember:
1 minute = 60 seconds
2 minutes = 120 seconds
3 minutes = 180 seconds

To rise from a depth of 0.2 km below sea level. Remember that 0.2 km = 200 m.

$$N = 6 \times 200 = 1200 \text{ seconds} = 20 \text{ minutes}$$

⟩GO FIGURE!

Calculate the appropriate amount of time you would need to ascend from different depths using the formula and making substitutions in the data given.

1 How many seconds, N, should you take to rise from a depth, D, of:
a) 9 m b) 40 m
c) 0.3 km d) 0.5 km
e) 600 m?

2 Write the times for b, c, d and e in minutes.

3 A fellow diver tells you she will rise from a depth of 400 m in 40 minutes. Is this correct?

4 If you take 24 seconds to ascend to the surface, what is the maximum depth you should have ascended from?

5 If you take 20 minutes and 12 seconds to ascend to the surface, what is the maximum depth you should have ascended from?

GO FIGURE! ANSWERS

04–05 Learning to dive

1. a) -40 is the deepest.
   b) -6, -18, -25, -32, -40
2. a) -35 + 10 = -25 m
   b) -25 – 17 = -42 m
3. 28 – 7 = 21 m
4. a) 31 – 3 = 28 m, b) 31 – 16 = 15 m
   c) 31 + 2 = 33 m

06–07 Coral reefs

1. They have all decreased in size.
2. a) 250 – 200 = 50 km²
   b) 320 – 224 = 96 km²
   c) 900 – 495 = 405 km²
3. Reef A: $^{50}/_{250}$ x 100 = 20%
   Reef B: $^{96}/_{320}$ x 100 = 30%
   Reef C: $^{405}/_{900}$ x 100 = 45%
4. Reef C's area has had the greatest percentage change.
5. 400,000 - 280,000 = 120,000 difference.
   So the percentage change is:

$$\frac{120,000}{400,000} \times 100 = 30\%$$

08–09 Shipwreck

1. a) (-4, 5) b) (-5, -3)
   c) (2, -5) d) (4, 0)
2. a) Treasure chest
   b) Musket (pistol)
3. (4, 2) (5, 2) (6, 2)
4. 8 squares left and 7 squares down
5. a) Treasure chest b) Cannon

10–11 Ocean bed

1. 1) -4400 m 2) -4000 m 3) -5800 m
   4) -6000 m 5) -7400 m 6) -8200 m
   7) -8000 m 8) -6400 m
2. a) 8200 – 4000 = 4,200 m
   b) 8000 – 6000 = 2,000 m
3. -4400 – 4000 – 5800 – 6000
   – 7400 – 8200 – 8000 – 6400
   = -50,200 ÷ 8 = -6275 m
4. Reading 8 is the most representative.

12–13 Submarine

1. a) 30 kph, b) -500 m, -3000 m, -5500 m
2. a) 80 psi b) 30 psi
3. 247,615 – 247,395 = 220 nautical miles
4. 12 – 7 = 5 hours
   220 ÷ 5 = 44 knots average speed

14–15 Watch out!

1. a) (5, 3) b) (3, 1) c) (-2, -4) d) (-4, -6)
2. No
3. y = x – 4
4. (4, 8) (1, 2) and (-1, -2)

16–17 Shoals and sharks

1. a) $^{15}/_{50}$ or $^{3}/_{10}$ b) $^{3}/_{10}$ = 0.3
2. a) $^{90}/_{100}$ or $^{9}/_{10}$ b) $^{9}/_{10}$ = 0.9
3. a) $^{36}/_{144}$ or $^{9}/_{36}$ or ¼ b) ¼ = 0.25

18–19 Sunken city

1. a) $(12 + 8) \times 2 = 40$ m b) $12 \times 8 = 96$ m^2

2. Long side: 7 m $- 4$m $= 3$ m
Short side: 5 m $- 3$ m $= 2$ m
Perimeter is $7 + 5 + 4 + 2 + 3 + 3 = 24$ m

3. $(5 \times 4) + (3 \times 3) = 20 + 9 = 29$ m^2 or
$(7 \times 3) + (4 \times 2) = 21 + 8 = 29$ m^2

4. The three unmarked sides add up to 10 m
(to match the length of the opposite side).
Perimeter is $10 + 3 + 3 + 6 + 10 + 6 = 38$ m

20–21 Wonderful whales

1. C) Surface area is 6×9 cm^2 $= 54$ cm^2
Volume is $3 \times 3 \times 3 = 27$ cm^3,
so ratio is 2:1
D) Surface area is 6×36 cm^2 $= 216$ cm^2
Volume is $6 \times 6 \times 6 = 216$ cm^3,
so ratio is 1:1
E) Surface area is 6×144 cm^2 $= 864$ cm^2
Volume is $12 \times 12 \times 12 = 1728$ cm^3,
so ratio is 1:2

2. a) D, b) A, c) E

3. Yes.

4. The larger the surface area is in relation to
the volume, the more surface they have to
lose their body heat through. Larger adults
have proportionally more inner space and
less surface area, so they lose less of their
body heat.

22–23 Billions of krill

1. a) 19,000,000
b) 900,000,000,000
c) 800,000,000,000,000

2. 490 billion

3. $19,000,000 = 1.9 \times 10^7$

4. a) Seven billion
b) 7×10^9 or 7.0×10^9

5. 8×10^{14} or 8.0×10^{14}

24–25 Underwater volcano

1. $6 \div 2 = 3$ km radius

2. $6 \times 3.14 =$ approximately 19 km
circumference

3. $(3 \times 3) \times 3.14 =$ approximately 28 km^2
area of the base

4. 700 m $= 0.7$ km

5. $\frac{1}{3} \times 3.14 \times (3 \times 3) \times 0.7 =$
approximately 7 km^3 volume of cone

6. $\frac{1}{3} \times 3.14 \times (110 \times 110) \times 6 =$
approximately 75,988 km^3
volume of cone

26–27 Don't get the bends

1. a) $9 \times 6 = 54$ seconds
b) $40 \times 6 = 240$ seconds
c) 0.3 km $= 300$ m,
so $300 \times 6 = 1800$ seconds
d) 0.5 km $= 500$ m,
so $500 \times 6 = 3000$ seconds
e) $600 \times 6 = 3600$ seconds

2. $240 \div 60 = 4$ minutes
$1800 \div 60 = 30$ minutes
$3000 \div 60 = 50$ minutes
$3600 \div 60 = 60$ minutes

3. $400 \times 6 = 2400$ seconds
$2400 \div 60 = 40$ minutes
So the answer is yes.

4. $24 \div 6 = 4$ m

5. 20 minutes 12 seconds $= 1212$ seconds
$1212 \div 6 = 202$ m

MATHS GLOSSARY

AREA
The amount of two-dimensional space covered by a shape or an object. For example, the area of a rectangle is calculated by multiplying the length of one of the short sides by the length of one of the long sides.

BILLION
A thousand million, sometimes written as 1.0×10^9.

CIRCUMFERENCE
The perimeter of a circle, the distance all the way around the edge.

CONE
A solid shape with a circular base and one point, or vertex.

COORDINATES
A series of numbers that will locate a point against axes.

DATA
A collection of facts or information.

DENOMINATOR
The bottom number in a fraction.

DIAMETER
The widest length across a circle, passing through the centre.

EQUATION
An expression with two sides to it that are linked with an equals symbol. Equations are solved by entering values.

FORMULA
An equation that shows the relationship between two different quantities. Its plural is formulae.

KNOT
A speed travelling at sea equivalent to 1 nautical mile per hour.

LINEAR GRAPH
Sometimes called a straight line graph, a graph that shows the relationship in which the amount goes up or down in the same increment each time, forming a straight line.

MEAN AVERAGE
A number found by adding all the values in a set of data and dividing by the number of values there are.

NEGATIVE NUMBER
A number that is less than zero. We write negative numbers using the minus sign (-), e.g. -5, -3, -7.

NUMERATOR
The top number in a fraction.

PERCENTAGE
A fraction with a denominator of 100.

PERIMETER
The total distance around a two-dimensional shape.

PI
The relationship between the diameter and circumference of a circle. It is written as π, and equal to roughly 3.14, or $^{22}\!/_{7}$.

POSITIVE NUMBER
A number that is greater than zero.

QUADRANT
One of the four sections created when a shape is divided by two lines that cross, such as the x-axis and y-axis.

RECTANGLE
A four-sided shape in which all four corners have an angle of 90°.

RADIUS
The distance between the centre of a circle and its edge.

RATIO
A way to show how a number or value is related to another. A ratio of 2:1 shows that there are twice as many of the first value as there are of the second.

SIMPLIFY/SIMPLEST FORM
To simplify a fraction we change to an equivalent fraction that uses smaller numbers, e.g. $^{6}\!/_{8} = $ ¾. When a number cannot be simplified, it is in its simplest form. Ratios can also be simplified in the same way: 4:12 = 1:3.

STANDARD FORM
A way of writing large numbers using powers of ten. Numbers are written in the form: ___ $\times 10^{x}$, such as 3.2×10^{6} or 7.25×10^{11}.

SURFACE AREA
The amount of two-dimensional space covered by the surface of an object. It is found by adding up the areas of all the object's sides.

TRILLION
A thousand billion, sometimes written as 1.0×10^{12}.

VALUE
The total amount that a number or group of numbers adds up to.

VOLUME
The amount of space an object takes up. It is measured in cubic units, such as cubic centimetres (cm^{3}) or cubic metres (m^{3}).

INDEX

32

WEBSITES

www.mathisfun.com
A huge website packed full of
explanations, examples, games,
puzzles, activities, worksheets
and teacher resources for all
age levels.

www.bbc.co.uk/bitesize
The revision section of the BBC
website, it contains tips and
easy-to-follow instructions on
all subjects, including maths,
as well as games and activities.

www.mathplayground.com
An action-packed website with
maths games, mathematical
word problems, worksheets,
puzzles and videos.

ACKNOWLEDGEMENTS

Published in paperback
in 2017 by Wayland

Copyright © Hodder and
Stoughton, 2017

All rights reserved

Editor: Elizabeth Brent
Produced by Tall Tree Ltd
Editors: Joe Fullman and
Rob Colson
Designer: Ed Simkins

ISBN: 9780750298490

Wayland, an imprint of Hachette Children's Group
Part of Hodder and Stoughton
Carmelite House
50 Victoria Embankment
London EC4Y 0DZ

An Hachette UK Company
www.hachette.co.uk
www.hachettechildrens.co.uk

Printed and bound in China

10 9 8 7 6 5 4 3 2 1

FSC

The website addresses (URLs) included in this book
were valid at the time of going to press. However, it
is possible that contents or addresses may have
changed since the publication of this book. No
responsibility for any such changes can be accepted
by either the author or the Publisher.

Picture credits
All istockphoto: 4-5 strmko, 6–7 VitalyEdush,
14–15 Snaprender, 22–23 Tenedos, 26-27 richcarey